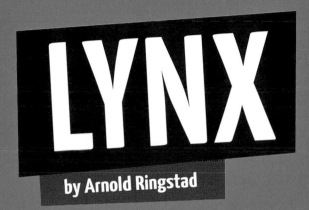

LYNX

by Arnold Ringstad

RiverStream Science

RiverStream Science
Great Reading • Real Learning

Amicus High Interest hardcover edition is published by Amicus
P.O. Box 1329, Mankato, MN 56002
www.amicuspublishing.us

Library of Congress Cataloging-in-Publication Data
Ringstad, Arnold.
  Lynx / by Arnold Ringstad.
    pages cm. -- (Wild cats)
  Includes index.
  Audience: Age 6.
  Audience: K to Grade 3.
  ISBN 978-1-60753-604-8 (hardcover) -- ISBN 978-1-60753-644-4 (pdf ebook)
  1. Lynx--Juvenile literature. I. Title.
  QL737.C23R568 2014
  599.75'3--dc23
                                        2013049793

Photo Credits: Pyshnyy Maxim Vjacheslavovich/Shutterstock Images, cover; mthaler/
Thinkstock, 2, 4–5; Critterbiz/Shutterstock Images, 6–7; Scott E Read/Shutterstock
Images, 8–9, 22; Ijdema/Thinkstock, 10–11; SuperStock/Glow Images, 12–13; Frank
Sommariva/ImageBroker/Glow Images, 14–15; imagebroker.net/SuperStock, 16–17;
Roland Ijdema/Shutterstock Images, 18–19, 23; Volodymyr Burdiak/Shutterstock Images,
20–21

Produced for Amicus by The Peterson Publishing Company
and Red Line Editorial.

Designer Becky Daum
Printed in the United States of America
Mankato, MN

19 20 21 CG 22 21 20
RiverStream Publishing–Corporate Graphics, Mankato, MN
ISBN 978-1-62243-252-3 (paperback)

TABLE OF CONTENTS

Cold Weather Cats   4

Furry Cats   6

Ears and Eyes   8

Awake at Night   10

Sneaking and Pouncing   12

Hiding Food   14

Lynx Cubs   16

Growing Up   18

Saving the Lynx   20

Lynx Facts   22

Words to Know   23

Learn More   24

Index   24

Cold Weather Cats

Lynx are wild cats from Asia and Europe. They live in snowy forests. Big paws help lynx walk in snow.

Furry Cats

Lynx fur is brown and white. Their fur has patterns. Some lynx have stripes. Others have spots. The cats have furry paws. Fur keeps their feet warm.

Like a Housecat?

Many housecats also have stripes or spots.

Ears and Eyes

Lynx have **tufts** of ear hair. This gives them good hearing. The cats also have good eyesight. They see **prey** far away.

Fun Fact

Lynx can see mice 250 feet (76 m) away.

Awake at Night

Lynx are **nocturnal**. They are awake at night. They hunt in the dark. The cats rest during the day. They sleep in tall grass or in forests. Sometimes they rest in trees.

Sneaking and Pouncing

Lynx hunt deer. They move quietly. Good eyes help them find prey. They **pounce** on the deer. Then the lynx bite their necks.

Fun Fact

Lynx have strong jaws. They can kill with one bite.

Hiding Food

Lynx cannot eat a whole deer. They hide extra meat. They put it in a tree. Other animals cannot find it. The lynx come back to eat it later.

Like a Housecat?

Some housecats hide their food.

Lynx Cubs

Lynx cubs are born in **dens**. Some dens are in logs. Others are between rocks. New cubs have folded ears. Their eyes are closed. Cubs' eyes open in ten days.

Growing Up

Lynx cubs drink milk. It comes from their mother. After four months they start eating meat. At ten months they live alone. Lynx are fully grown in two years.

Saving the Lynx

People once hunted lynx. They became rare. Scientists helped lynx in the 1970s. They brought cats to old habitats. Now the lynx are doing better.

Lynx Facts

Size: 40–75 pounds (18–36 kg), 28–51 inches (70–130 cm)

Range: Northern Europe and Asia

Habitat: rocky areas, forests

Number of babies: 1–5

Food: deer

Special feature: large, furry paws

Words to Know

dens – places animals use for shelter

nocturnal – active at night

pounce – to jump on

prey – animals hunted by other animals

tufts – bunches of hair

Learn More

Books

Parker, Barbara Keevil and Duane F. Parker. *Lynxes (Early Bird Nature Books)*. Minneapolis, MN: Lerner Publications, 2005.

Randall, Henry. *Lynxes (Cats of the Wild)*. New York: PowerKids Press, 2011.

Websites

National Geographic—Lynx

http://animals.nationalgeographic.com/animals/mammals/lynx

See photos of lynx and hear the sounds they make.

San Diego Zoo—Lynx and Bobcat

http://animals.sandiegozoo.org/animals/lynx-and-bobcat

Learn about the lynx that live at the San Diego Zoo.

Index

cubs, 17, 19

ears, 9, 17

forests, 5, 11
fur, 6

housecats, 6, 15
hunting, 11, 12

paws, 5, 6
prey, 9, 12, 14

scientists, 21
sleeping, 11

trees, 11, 14